Read and Play
Ships

by Jim Pipe

Aladdin/Watts
London • Sydney

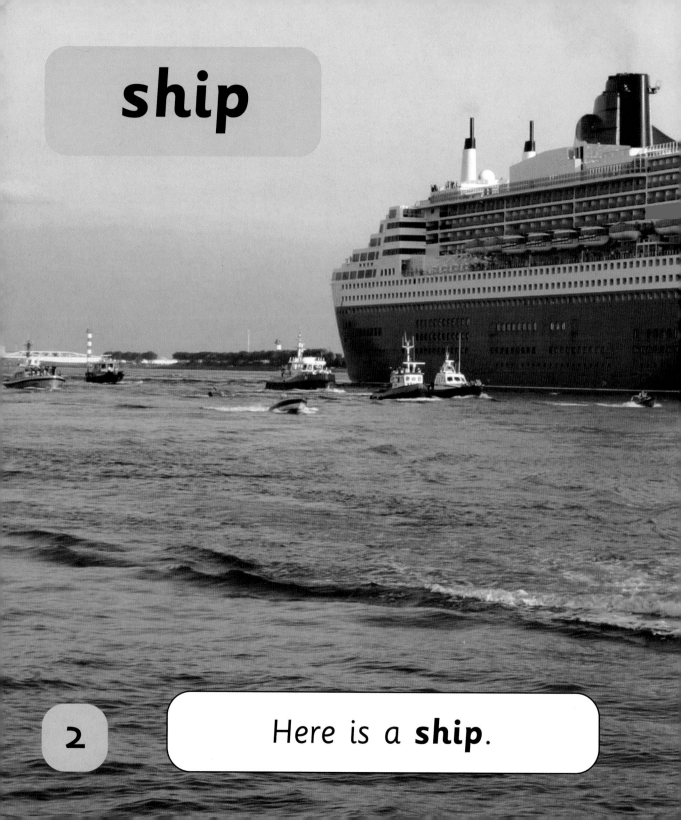

ship

2

Here is a **ship**.

A **ship** is a big boat.

3

hull

A ship has a **hull**.

This ship has two **hulls**.

deck

This ship has a big **deck**.

6

Planes land
on the **deck**.

7

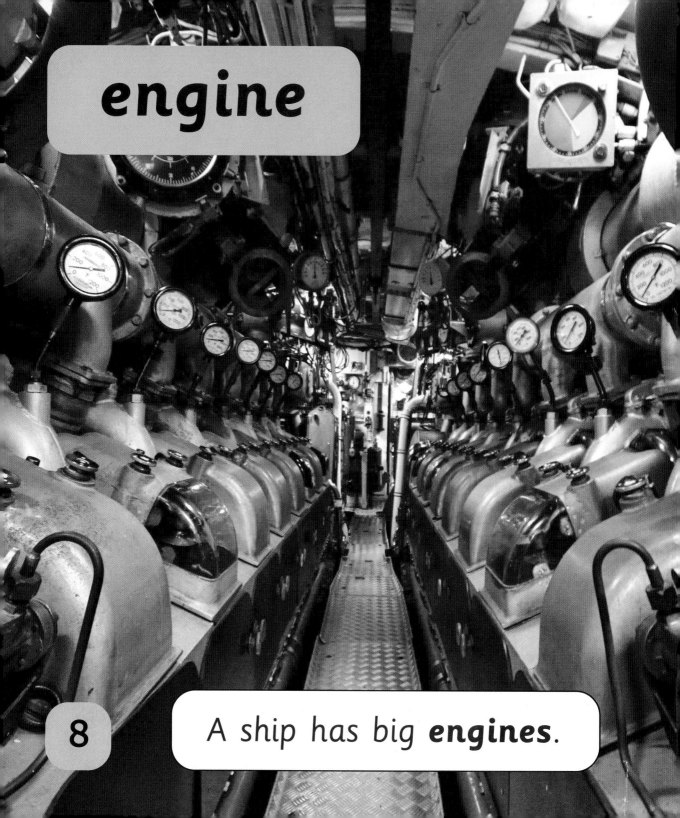

engine

A ship has big **engines**.

propeller

Engines turn a **propeller**.

sails

This ship has **sails**.

Sails make a ship move.

11

sailor

12

Sailors sail a ship.

anchor

A ship drops its **anchor** to stop.

13

port

14

A ship stops in a **port**.

Ships are safe in a **port**.

15

fishing

A **fishing** boat is small.

tanker

A **tanker** is enormous.

submarine

This is a **submarine**.

18

It can go
underwater.

What am I?

anchor

hull

propeller

sails

20

Match the words and pictures.

How many?

Can you count the red ships?

21

What job?

Tanker

Cargo ship

Ferry

Fishing boat

What jobs do these ships do?

Index

Can you find these
pictures of ships
in this book?

For Parents and Teachers

Questions you could ask:

p. 2 Where would you see a ship? e.g. at sea, in a port, on a big river. Ask what boats/ships the reader has seen, e.g. ferry, yacht, canoe, pirate ship.

p. 4 What are ships made from? Ships today are made of metal. In the past ships were made of wood.

p. 6 What is this ship called? It is called an aircraft carrier because it carries aircraft. It has a very big deck so that planes can land on it. Most ships have a deck, the flat part on top of a ship that you can walk on, e.g. the deck on a ferry.

p. 9 What makes a big ship move? The engines make the propeller spin. This pushes a ship forward. To go backwards, the propellers spin the other way.

p.10 How many sails can you see? Explain how sails work: when the wind blows against a sail, it pushes a boat forward. Ask the reader to blow a feather or a ping pong ball across a bowl of water.

p. 13 What is an anchor for? A heavy anchor sinks to the bottom and stops a ship from floating away.

p. 14 What can you see in a port? e.g. tall cranes to unload cargo, tug helping a big ship to dock.

p.18 If you were in a submarine underwater, what could you see? Ask reader to describe what is under the water, e.g. sea animals, seabed.

Activities you could do:

• Ask readers to describe or imagine a journey in a boat, e.g. wind and waves, rocking of the boat, sounds, getting splashed! You could use this as an opportunity to discuss water safety.

• Encourage puddle or water play, e.g. watching ripples/waves, seeing what objects float or sink and testing how deep water is using a stick.

• Role play: Get readers to sit in a circle and "row" a boat while singing: "Row, row, row your boat".

• Help the reader to cut out or collect pictures of different boats, e.g. fishing boats, pirate ships.

• Make boats/rafts from plastic plates, egg cartons, paper. Explore which materials work best.

© Aladdin Books Ltd 2007

Designed and produced by
Aladdin Books Ltd
2/3 Fitzroy Mews
London W1T 6DF

First published in 2007
in Great Britain
by Franklin Watts
338 Euston Road
London NW1 3BH

Franklin Watts Australia
Level 17/207 Kent Street
Sydney NSW 2000

Franklin Watts is a division of Hachette Children's Books.

ISBN 978 0 7496 7503 5

A catalogue record for this book is available from the British Library.

Dewey Classification: 387.2

Printed in Malaysia
All rights reserved

Series consultant
Zoe Stillwell is an experienced Early Years teacher currently teaching at Pewley Down Infant School, Guildford.

Photocredits:
l-left, r-right, b-bottom, t-top, c-centre, m-middle
All photos from istockphoto.com except: 5, 23 mtl — Richard Bennett, Courtesy Incat. 12, 13, 6-7, 18-19, 20br, 23br — US Navy. 21 — Courtesy Superfast Ferries.